A NEW OWL BIBLE STORY BOOK

David the shepherd boy

Illustrated by Gordon Stowell

Scripture Union

47 Marylebone Lane, London W1M 6AX, England.

Christian Literature Crusade

Fort Washington, Pennsylvania 19034, U.S.A.

First published in this form 1977.

David was the youngest boy in a family of eight.

His job was to
look after the sheep.

Where David lived
there were wild animals.
God helped David
to be brave and to
take care of the sheep.

One day he saw
a big lion.
It was prowling around
the sheep,
ready to attack.

David moved quickly.
He put a stone
in his sling,
swung it in a circle,
and hurled the stone
through the air.

The stone hit the lion
and killed it.
The sheep were safe now
that the lion was dead.

On another day
a big bear crept softly
up to David.

David killed the bear, too.

David said,
'God loves me.
He looks after me
and helps me to
look after the sheep.'

David loved God.
He often made up songs
to say
thank you to God.

When David grew up,
the people wanted him
to be king
because he loved God
and was so brave.

God loves us
and we
can love him, too.

You can find this story in 1 Samuel chapter 17.